CRAFTY
IDEAS FROM
JUNK

For my sister Shirley

Published in Great Britain in 1990 by
Exley Publications Ltd, 16 Chalk Hill,
Watford, Herts WD1 4BN, United Kingdom.
Reprinted 1990

Text copyright © Myrna Daitz, 1990
Illustrations copyright © Gillian Chapman, 1990

British Library Cataloguing in Publication Data
Daitz, Myrna.
  Crafty ideas from junk.
  1. Handicrafts using scrap materials.
  I. Title.
  II. Gillian Chapman.
  745.58′4

ISBN 1-85015-191-1

Series designers: Gillian Chapman and Linda Sullivan.
"Mad Robot" (page 34) and "French Knitting Slippers"
(page 63) designed by Gillian Chapman.
Editorial: Margaret Montgomery.
Typeset by Brush Off Studios, St Albans, Herts AL3 4PH.
Printed and bound in Hungary.

CRAFTY
IDEAS FROM
JUNK

Myrna Daitz

Pictures
by
Gillian Chapman

EXLEY

In the same series:

Crafty Ideas From Nature
Crafty Ideas For Presents

Coming in Autumn 1990:

Crafty Ideas For Parties

Contents

Introduction

ENVIRONMENT FRIENDLY!

Crafty Ideas from Junk contains over forty projects for young children of five to ten years, all using scrap materials. Everything in the book can be made from bits and pieces you can find around the house. Packets, tins, cartons, milk bottle tops (previously sterilized) and egg boxes provide endless creative potential. Old material, wallpaper oddments, pieces of polystyrene, newspapers and old computer paper can all be used creatively.

Children can experiment with cutting and sticking boxes together to make so many different things. They will benefit from the use of scissors, and a great deal of concentration is developed when fitting and measuring items together. Fitting the different sizes and shapes together helps develop mathematical concepts.

When working at junk modelling the children explore ideas – they reason – judge – and draw conclusions. In fact, they learn to *think*.

Children will benefit from the artistic creations they produce, and they will build confidence. The less creative child need not be distressed if something he or she makes does not turn out correctly, as failures can be discarded at no cost, and started again.

When children see how many boxes and packets an average family discards, they will start to appreciate the need for conservation, learn how much we waste and begin to think about what we are doing to our environment.

So before you are tempted to throw away your empty packets and boxes, think of their educational potential and help your child to create something with them.

Happy sticking.

Shapes from Junk

What you need:–
Round cheese carton.
Empty food boxes and packets.
Paint and a brush.
Scissors.
Glue.
A pencil.   A ruler.
A scrap book.

triangle

circle

1. Cut out circles, triangles, rectangles and squares from the boxes and packets. Make each shape in several different sizes.

rectangle

square

2. Paint all the shapes brightly.

3. Try to make pictures using the shapes. Clowns, children and engines are all easy to make from shapes.

4. When you have decided on your shape picture glue it carefully into your scrap book. Write underneath each shape how you made your picture.

train

Parent's Handy Hints :—
This is an excellent lesson in shape. Help your child to draw and cut out all the shapes in different sizes.
Talk about the name of each shape.
They must write on each page what shapes they used.

I used
1 triangle
2 rectangles
3 squares
for my house

house

3-Dimensional Tube Pictures

1. Cover the toilet roll tubes with gummed paper, using a variety of shades.

What you need :-
Cardboard tubes.
Assorted gummed paper.
Polystyrene ceiling tiles.
Cotton tape.
Adhesive tape.
Wallpaper paste.
Scissors.

2. Cut the covered tubes into different sizes.

3. Stand the tubes on the tile, and when you have decided on an interesting pattern, glue the rims of the tubes on to the tile.

Parent's Handy Hint :-
Now you know what to do with all those left over ceiling tiles !

4. Using the adhesive tape, stick the cotton tape to the top of the tile so that you can hang your picture up with it.

Bedroom Name Plates

What you need :-

Old magazines.
Cardboard.
Pieces of tissue paper.
Blu-tack.
Glue and a brush.
Scissors.

1. Cut out large letters from the magazines.

2. Measure and cut the card to the size you want for your bedroom door.

3. Sort the letters. Find all the letters in your name and carefully glue them on to the cardboard.

4. To decorate the edges of the cardboard, crumple up small pieces of tissue paper and glue firmly on.

5. Put the blu-tack on the back of the cardboard and press the nameplate firmly on to your door.

Parent's Handy Hints :-
This can keep children busy for hours. It is very good for them to sort out the letters. Help them to cut out small apostrophe's to assemble their names.

P G M

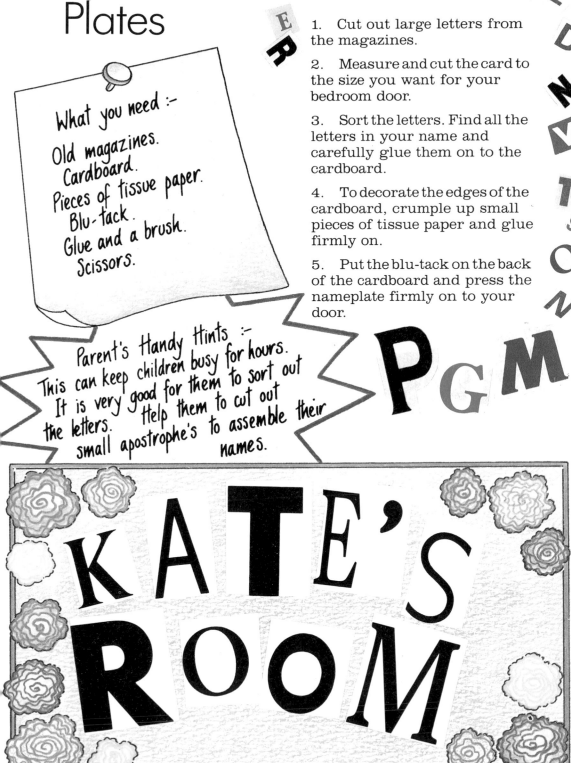

KATE'S ROOM

A Balloon Cat

What you need :—
2 round balloons.
Lots of old newspaper.
Flour.   String.
Water.
Glue.
Old pieces of material.
Small pieces of wool.
Scissors.
Paint and paint brush.

1.   Blow up the two balloons. Make one large and one medium sized. Tie a string to the end of each balloon.

2.   Make a thick paste with the flour and water.

3.   Tear the newspapers into long thin strips. Dip some of the strips into water and cover one balloon by criss-crossing the wet strips all over it. Leave the string uncovered.

4.   Now dip more paper strips into the thick paste you have made and cover the balloon with these.

5.   Repeat the pasted layers several times until the balloon is large and solid. Hang it up by the string to dry.

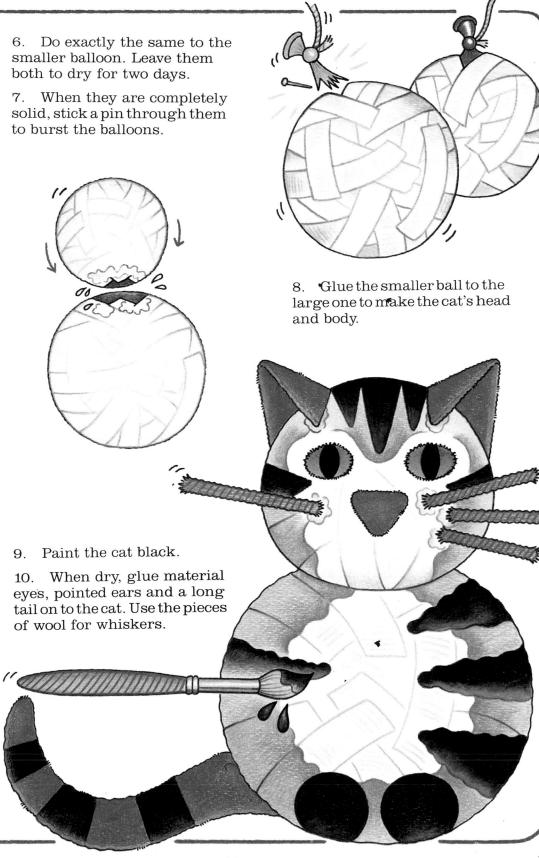

6. Do exactly the same to the smaller balloon. Leave them both to dry for two days.

7. When they are completely solid, stick a pin through them to burst the balloons.

8. Glue the smaller ball to the large one to make the cat's head and body.

9. Paint the cat black.

10. When dry, glue material eyes, pointed ears and a long tail on to the cat. Use the pieces of wool for whiskers.

15

A Xylophone

1. Fill the first bottle with water almost to the top.

2. Fill the second one halfway.

What you need:—
8 empty bottles of the same size & shape.

Water.
A fork.

3. Put just a little water in the third, and continue this way until each bottle has a different level of water in it.

4. Using the fork, hit each bottle gently. By experimenting with the different sounds, and moving the bottles around, tunes can be played.

Parent's Handy Hints:—
This is a great party game for all the family. You can also teach your child the names of the musical notes.

Do   Ray   Me   Fah   So   La   Tee   Do

A Tin Can Printer

1. Remove both ends of the can and cover the jagged edges with insulating tape to protect yourself from cuts.

What you need :—
Empty food cans.
Thick poster paint.
Very thick twine.
A deep plate.
Glue.
Insulating tape.
Paper.

2. Place the twine around the can in a nice shape. When you have decided on the shape, glue the twine into place.

3. Make sure the glue is dry and the twine very secure before you start painting.

Parent's Handy Hints :—
Always make sure cans are clean & jagged edges are covered. The twine can be cut up & glued on to the can in pieces.

4. Put some paint into the deep plate and roll the can in the paint. The paint will stick to the twine but not to the can.

5. Roll the can over a sheet of paper and the twine will print the shapes.

Book Ends

What you need :-
Empty food packets in all different sizes.
Paint & a brush.
Strong glue.
Dried beans.
Adhesive tape.

Parent's Handy Hints :-
Any size of box, packet or carton can be used for this project.
WARN young children not to eat the dried beans.

1.   Fill the packets with the dried beans to weigh them down, then seal them carefully at both ends with adhesive tape.

2.   Paint all the packets brightly. Leave to dry.

32.   Glue 4 of the packets together from the tallest to the smallest. Repeat with the other 4 packets. You now have a pair of smart book ends.

A String Holder

What you need :–

A ball of string.
Scissors.
Adhesive tape.
Felt tipped pens.
A paper plate.

1. Decorate a paper plate with felt-tipped pens.

2. Cut the plate in half. Each half will make one string holder.

3. Twist a half of the plate into a cone shape and tape it together with the sticky tape.

4. Cut off the point of the cone to make a hole for the string to go through.

5. Make a loop from a piece of string. Tape the loop to the top of the holder so that it will hang on a wall.

6. Put the ball of string into the cone with the end of the string coming out of the hole in the bottom.

Parent's Handy Hint :–
These make useful presents & can hang in a garage or greenhouse.
It does stop string getting in a tangle !

A Fir Cone Weather Bird

1. Draw 2 large bird's heads on the cardboard.

2. Cut them out.

3. Paint the heads and give the bird an eye and a beak.

What you need :-

A very large fir cone.
Pipe cleaners.
Thick card board.
Paint and paint brush.
Glue.
A pencil.
Scissors.

You can use this picture as a pattern for your bird's head.

4. Glue the heads together over a pipe cleaner neck.

5. When the head and neck are dry, push the pipe cleaner inside the cone making it as firm as you can.

6. Press two more pipe cleaners into the cone to make the legs. Twist the bottom of the pipe cleaners to make feet so that the weather bird can stand up.

Parent's Handy Hint :—
The fir cone should open its scales in fine weather and close them in wet weather.

Butterfly Plant Holder

1. Draw two identical butterfly shapes from the thick cardboard.

2. Cut them both out.

3. Decorate them both on one side, using as many different shades as possible.

You can use this picture as a pattern for your butterfly !

4. Glue them together, with the decorated side outward, *over* the top of the stick.

5. Leave to dry.

Parent's Handy Hints:-

These attractive plant holders are ideal for supporting house plants. The butterflies look very decorative peeping out of the flower pot. Tie the plant to the stick with cotton or gardening twine.

Papier Maché Plant Pot

What you need :-

Lots of old newspaper.
A plant pot.
Petroleum jelly.
Clear varnish.
Paint and paint brush.
Wallpaper paste and paste brush.

Parent's Handy Hints :-

It is best to let the children tear the newspaper into very tiny pieces.
If the paper is cut with scissors it does not work as well.

1. Tear the newspaper up into very tiny pieces.

2. Spread a thin layer of petroleum jelly over the outside of the plant pot.

3. Stick pieces of newspaper all over the greased outside of the pot, until it is completely covered.

4. Mix the packet of wallpaper paste and then brush it over all the newspaper on the plant pot.

5. Wait until it is *almost* dry, then cover it again with more scraps of newspaper.

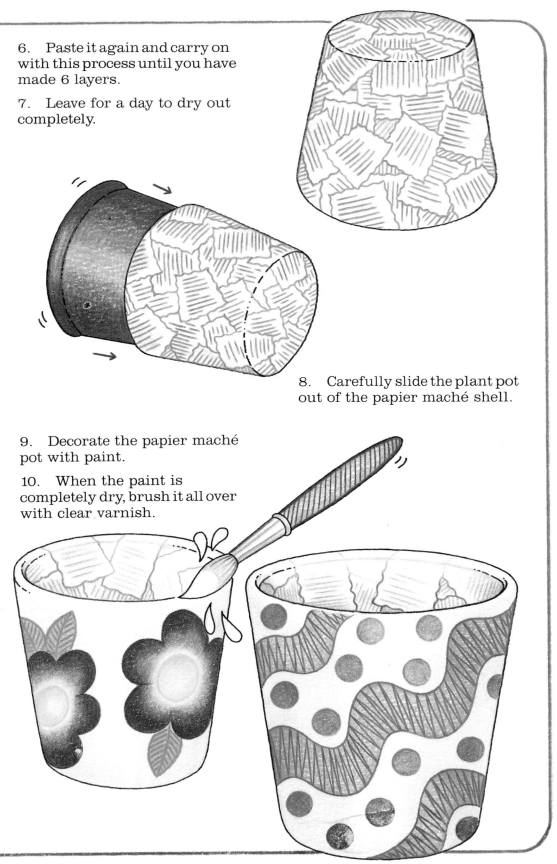

6.   Paste it again and carry on with this process until you have made 6 layers.

7.   Leave for a day to dry out completely.

8.   Carefully slide the plant pot out of the papier mâché shell.

9.   Decorate the papier mâché pot with paint.

10.   When the paint is completely dry, brush it all over with clear varnish.

Decorated
Table Mats

What you need :-
Assorted paper.
Large pieces of cardboard.
Scissors.
Glue.
Clear varnish & brush.

1. Cut or tear all the paper into very small pieces.

2. Cut the cardboard into large squares, triangles and circles.

3. Brush glue all around the **edges** of the shapes.

4. Lay the small pieces of **paper** around the edges of the shapes.

5. Leave to dry.

6. Paint the decorated edges **with** clear varnish.

Parent's Handy Hints :-
You will need to help your child to cut out the squares, triangles and circles.
Making your child aware of these shapes is good early mathematical training!

New Doilies from Old

What you need :-
Used cake doilies.
Paint and a brush.
White paper.
Scissors.

Parent's Handy Hint :-
This is a good way of using up old doilies. They look very nice & can be used.

1. Place the doily on the piece of white paper.

2. Thickly paint all over the doily. (It doesn't matter if the paint goes over the doily on to the paper.)

3. Carefully peel off the doily and throw it away. You now have a brand new doily.

4. When the new doily is dry, cut it out carefully following the outside edge of the pattern.

Bumpy Dough Pictures

Parent's Handy Hints :-
I think parents will enjoy this project as much as their children. Try to encourage the child to be realistic, e.g. green dough for grass, blue for sky, etc.

1.   Mix the flour and salt with a few spoonfuls of water. Mix very well and keep adding water slowly until the mixture is a soft dough.

2.   Share the dough out between your small bowls.

3.   Put a spoonful of paint in each bowl and mix gently into the dough until you have several bright doughs.

4. Using a pencil, draw the picture you want on the cardboard.

5. Now start building up your picture, using the different doughs.

To finish the picture press the sticky tape all around the edge of the picture to make a border.

Silhouettes

1. Using the blu-tack, put the white paper on the wall.

2. Ask a friend to sit in front of the paper.

3. Shine a bright light on to your friend and a shadow will show clearly on the paper.

4. Draw all around the shadow with a pencil.

5. Remove the paper and cut out the silhouette.

6. Glue the white silhouette on to the black paper, being sure the black paper is larger than the white so that the silhouette has a black border.

What you need :-
A large piece of white paper.
A large piece of black paper.
A bright reading lamp.
Glue.
A pencil.
Scissors.
Blu-tack.

A scrapbook can be made with silhouettes of all the family.

Felt Flower Bracelet

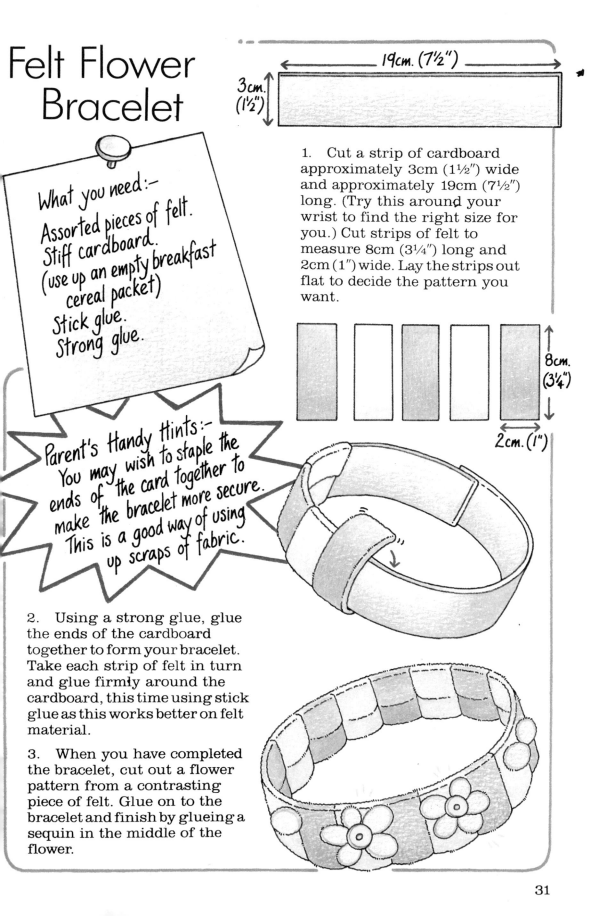

19cm. (7½")

3cm. (1½")

1. Cut a strip of cardboard approximately 3cm (1½") wide and approximately 19cm (7½") long. (Try this around your wrist to find the right size for you.) Cut strips of felt to measure 8cm (3¼") long and 2cm (1") wide. Lay the strips out flat to decide the pattern you want.

8cm. (3¼")

2cm. (1")

What you need:—
Assorted pieces of felt.
Stiff cardboard.
(use up an empty breakfast cereal packet)
Stick glue.
Strong glue.

Parent's Handy Hints:—
You may wish to staple the ends of the card together to make the bracelet more secure.
This is a good way of using up scraps of fabric.

2. Using a strong glue, glue the ends of the cardboard together to form your bracelet. Take each strip of felt in turn and glue firmly around the cardboard, this time using stick glue as this works better on felt material.

3. When you have completed the bracelet, cut out a flower pattern from a contrasting piece of felt. Glue on to the bracelet and finish by glueing a sequin in the middle of the flower.

Paper Bag Masks

What you need :-
Large paper bags
(NOT POLYTHENE)   Silver foil.
Glue.
Paints or crayons.
Ping pong balls.
2 small garden canes.
Odd pieces of wool and fabric.
Round empty cheese boxes.
Bristles from an old sweeping
        brush.

1.   Put the paper bag over your head and shoulders and ask an adult to mark the places that need to be cut out for your eyes and nose. Cut these out carefully.

Here are some ideas for decorating your masks:

1.   FOR A CAT. Draw a funny cat's face, make pointed paper ears and glue them in place. Glue on thick bristles for whiskers. Make a small bow tie from fabric and glue in place.

Brush bristle ⟶
    whiskers.

WARNING!
Make sure the bags are thin paper and use this opportunity to teach young children that polythene bags should NEVER be put over the head!

32

Ping-pong balls.

2. FOR A ROBOT. Glue on round empty cheese boxes covered in silver foil for the monster's eyes. Cover the garden canes with silver foil and tape on the sides of the face for antennae. Cut out a large square mouth.

Cheese carton eyes.

Ping-pong ball nose.

Parent's Handy Hint :–
Paper bag masks stimulate the imagination; provide the children with bags, material, wool, egg boxes, etc. and let them create their own characters.

3. FOR A CLOWN. Make fancy hair from strips of bright paper. Draw a large toothy grin. For the nose, paint a ping pong ball red and glue it on when dry. Paint the cheeks red.

Mad Robot

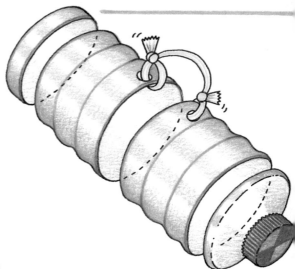

What you need :-
2 large cardboard boxes (1 head size & 1 body size)
2 cardboard tubes.
4 large empty plastic drink bottles.
2 plastic detergent bottle lids.
1 empty plastic margarine tub.
Old rubber gloves.
Scraps of coloured wire for hair.
Assorted bottle tops & lids.
Elastic, Glue, Scissors, Paints.

1. Cut off the flaps on the head-size cardboard box so you can put it over your head. Make 2 eyeholes.

2. Cut off the flaps on the body-size cardboard box. Make large holes in the sides for arm holes and a hole in the top large enough for your head to fit through.

Parent's Handy Hint :-
Large cardboard boxes are available at supermarkets.

3. Cut the large plastic drink bottles into sections. These must be no less than 13cm (5″) in diameter. To make the arm coverings join 2 sections together and attach to the cardboard body using the elastic. For the leg coverings just slide one section onto each leg. Cut one section into half lengthways and cover the shoe with it, keeping it in place with elastic.

4. Glue the 2 long cardboard tubes onto the head to make antennae and poke the pieces of wire through the cardboard for hair. Glue the 2 plastic detergent bottle lids to the side of the head for ears and glue the margarine tub to the face for a mouth.

5. Glue the assorted bottle tops and lids onto the robot's chest to make the control panel. The gauntlets can be made by cutting old rubber gloves down to size. The whole outfit can be painted.

35

Paper Plate Mask

What you need :-

A paper plate.
String or tape.
A pencil.
Scissors.
Felt tipped pens.
Strands of wool (for hair).
Glue.

1.   Put the paper plate in front of your face and ask an adult to mark the correct place for the eyeholes.

2.   Cut out two eyeholes.

3.   Draw a funny face on the mask, then decorate it with felt-tipped pens.

4.   Make a small hole on each side of the mask near the edge of the plate. These two holes should be just a little higher than the eyeholes.

5.   Tie the tape from one hole to the other. Put the string round the back of your head to hold the mask.

Parent's Handy Hints :-
Some very young children do not like the restriction of string or tape around their heads. In this case, glue the mask onto a small plant stick.
Masks can be made for theme parties – eg. Halloween.

Paper Chain Decorations

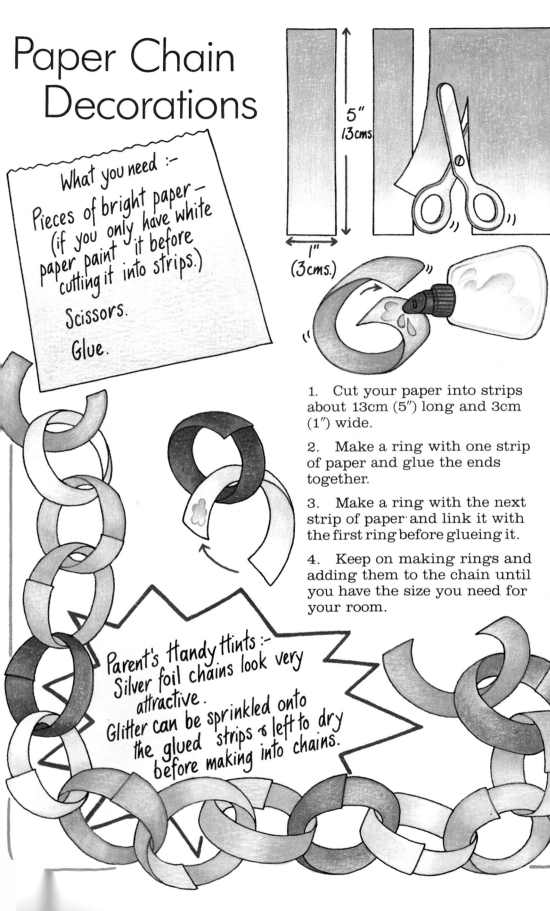

What you need :-
Pieces of bright paper – (if you only have white paper paint it before cutting it into strips.)

Scissors.

Glue.

5"
13cms.

1"
(3cms.)

1.   Cut your paper into strips about 13cm (5") long and 3cm (1") wide.

2.   Make a ring with one strip of paper and glue the ends together.

3.   Make a ring with the next strip of paper and link it with the first ring before glueing it.

4.   Keep on making rings and adding them to the chain until you have the size you need for your room.

Parent's Handy Hints :-
Silver foil chains look very attractive.
Glitter can be sprinkled onto the glued strips & left to dry before making into chains.

Hand Puppets

What you need :-
An old large sock.
Scraps of fabric.
2 buttons.
Glue.
Needle & thread.
Scissors.
Felt pens.

Parent's Handy Hints :-
Many different puppets can be made in this very easy way, e.g. animals, monsters, dinosaurs!

1. Put your hand into the foot of the sock, placing your fingers in the toe part, and your thumb in the heel.

2. Now push in the sole part of the sock to form the mouth of your puppet.

3. Ask someone to mark out exactly where the ears, nose and eyes should be on your puppet.

Save buttons and old scraps of fabric, and make hats & scarfs for the puppets.

4. Cut out the ears and tongue from the scraps of fabric and a small circle of red fabric for a nose. Stitch buttons on for eyes.

Children love to act out little plays & stories with puppets. They are very good for stimulating imagination & helping vocabulary.
A puppet show could be made from a large cardboard box.

Puppet Show

A Space Rocket

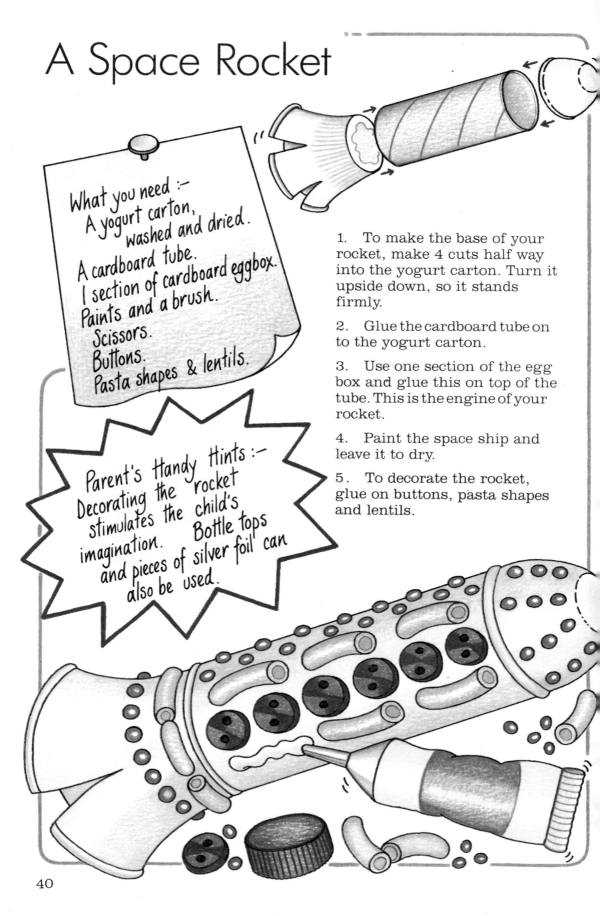

What you need :-
  A yogurt carton,
      washed and dried.
  A cardboard tube.
  I section of cardboard eggbox.
  Paints and a brush.
  Scissors.
  Buttons.
  Pasta shapes & lentils.

Parent's Handy Hints :-
Decorating the rocket
stimulates the child's
imagination.   Bottle tops
and pieces of silver foil can
      also be used.

1.   To make the base of your rocket, make 4 cuts half way into the yogurt carton. Turn it upside down, so it stands firmly.

2.   Glue the cardboard tube on to the yogurt carton.

3.   Use one section of the egg box and glue this on top of the tube. This is the engine of your rocket.

4.   Paint the space ship and leave it to dry.

5.   To decorate the rocket, glue on buttons, pasta shapes and lentils.

A Boomerang

What you need :-
2 large flat ice-lolly sticks.

Thin string or a strong rubber band.

1. **Cross** the two ice-lolly sticks as shown in the picture.

2. Tie them tightly into position with the string or rubber band.

Parent's Handy Hints :-
Teach your child how to toss the boomerang with a flick of the wrist so that it spins. It will then come back to you. The sticks can be decorated to look like real boomerangs.

Stilts

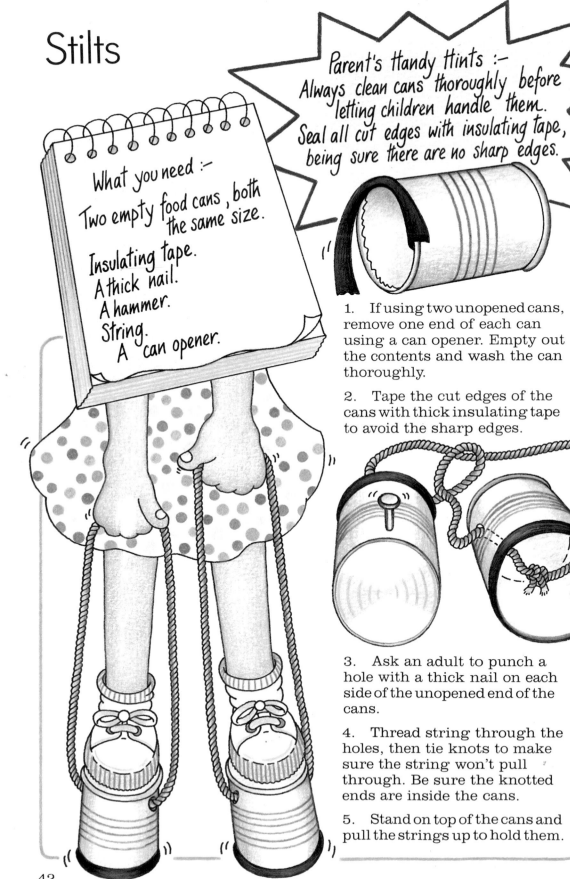

What you need :—

Two empty food cans, both the same size.

Insulating tape.
A thick nail.
A hammer.
String.
A can opener.

Parent's Handy Hints :— Always clean cans thoroughly before letting children handle them. Seal all cut edges with insulating tape, being sure there are no sharp edges.

1. If using two unopened cans, remove one end of each can using a can opener. Empty out the contents and wash the can thoroughly.

2. Tape the cut edges of the cans with thick insulating tape to avoid the sharp edges.

3. Ask an adult to punch a hole with a thick nail on each side of the unopened end of the cans.

4. Thread string through the holes, then tie knots to make sure the string won't pull through. Be sure the knotted ends are inside the cans.

5. Stand on top of the cans and pull the strings up to hold them.

Shell Boats

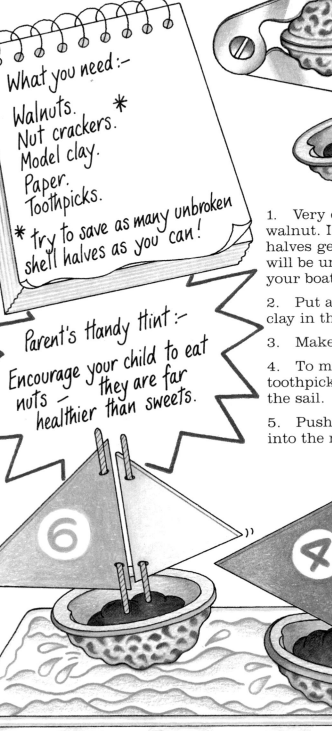

What you need :-

Walnuts.
Nut crackers. *
Model clay.
Paper.
Toothpicks.

* try to save as many unbroken shell halves as you can!

Parent's Handy Hint :-

Encourage your child to eat nuts – they are far healthier than sweets.

1. Very carefully crack a walnut. If you prise the two halves gently apart, one half will be unbroken. Use this for your boat.

2. Put a small piece of model clay in the shell.

3. Make sails from the paper.

4. To make the masts, put a toothpick in, out and through the sail.

5. Push the masts and sails into the model clay.

Cotton Spool Monster

What you need :-
As many empty cotton spools as possible, in all shapes & sizes. Paints & paint brush. A long piece of thick string.

1. Decorate each cotton spool in different patterns.

2. Decorate the largest spool to look like a head with eyes on it.

3. Make a very large knot at one end of the string to stop the spools falling off.

4. When they are all dry, thread the spools on to the string, leaving the head of the monster until the last.

Parent's Handy Hint :-
Collecting the cotton spools can be fun and sorting & classifying them is good early mathematical training.

Two-way Talking Telephone

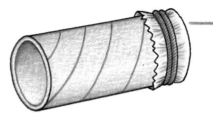

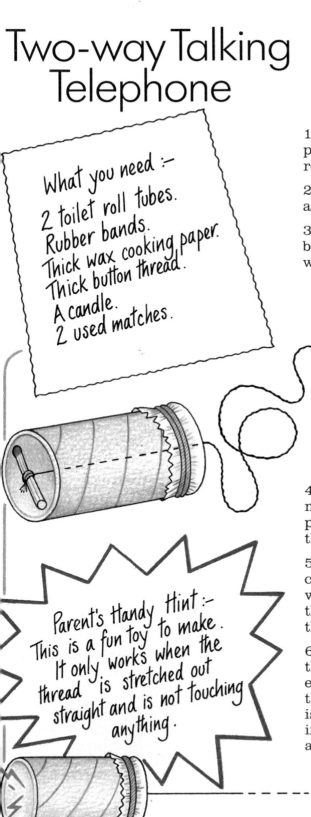

What you need :-
2 toilet roll tubes.
Rubber bands.
Thick wax cooking paper.
Thick button thread.
A candle.
2 used matches.

Parent's Handy Hint :-
This is a fun toy to make.
It only works when the
thread is stretched out
straight and is not touching
anything.

1. Stretch a piece of waxed paper over one end of each toilet roll tube.

2. Keep the paper in place with a thick rubber band.

3. Cut a very long piece of button thread and rub all over it with the candle to wax it.

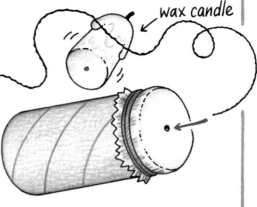

wax candle

4. Make a tiny hole in the middle of the waxed paper then push the thread down through the hole.

5. Tie a match to the piece that comes through the hole. This will keep the thread in place so that it won't pull back through the hole.

6. Attach the other end of the thread to the other tube in exactly the same way. Pull the thread tight and your telephone is ready to use. When you speak into one end, you can be heard at the other end.

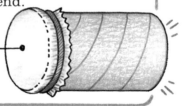

1-2-3-4 Fishing Game

Use this shape for your fish!

What you need :-

A large, sturdy carton.
Thin cardboard.
Paper clips.
Thick button thread.
Plant sticks.
Scissors.
Paints and a paint brush.
Black felt-tipped pen.

Parent's Handy Hints :-

This is a good game for helping to learn numbers. Each competitor has six turns and then the numbers on each of their captured fish are added up. The highest scorer is the winner!

1. Cut out 20 fish shapes from the thin cardboard. Paint them in different shades.

2. With the black felt-tipped pen, put numbers on the fishes. Mark all the red ones number 1; all the blue ones number 2; all the green ones number 3 and all the yellow ones number 4.

3. Open out one end of a paper-clip and pull it gently round until it is an S shape.

4. Hook one end through the nose of a fish and the other end through a second S shaped paper-clip. Tie the second paper-clip on to a long piece of thread and then tie the other end of the thread on to a plant stick.

5. Put all your fish into the carton, and then "fish" for them by trying to hook a paper-clip with the paper-clip on the end of your fishing line.

The "pond" carton can be painted with a fishy picture.

47

Board Game

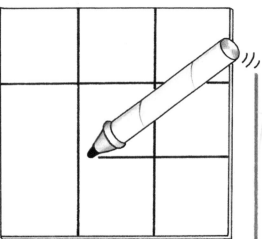

1. Mark off 4 thick lines with a black felt-tipped pen on the cardboard. Two should go across and two should go up and down. You should now have 9 even-sized squares.

2. Cut 10 small even-sized cards. On five pieces draw circles and on the other five pieces draw crosses. Use one shade of felt-tipped pen for the circles and a different shade for the crosses. You are now ready to play the game.

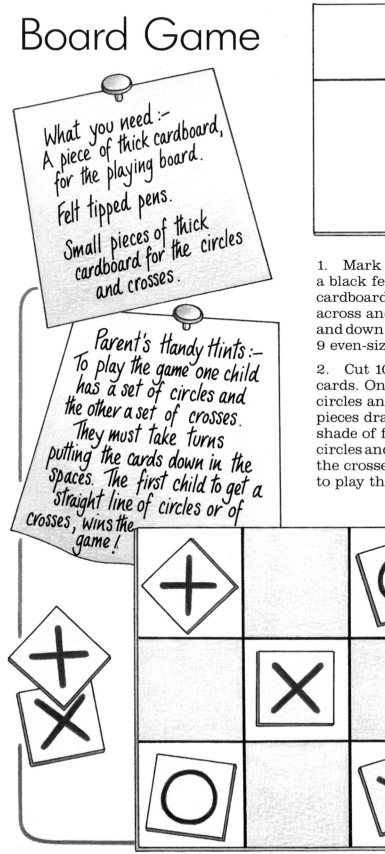

Jigsaws

1. Cut out attractive pictures from magazines. Glue them on to thick cardboard, pressing out any air bubbles.

2. When dry, brush the picture with clear varnish.

3. When the varnish is completely dry, cut out as many puzzle pieces as you can, making them into interesting shapes.

4. Keep the puzzles in separate envelopes to avoid mixing them up. Label the envelopes with a description of the picture.

Parent's Handy Hints :-

To make the jigsaws last longer, use thick cardboard.
You may have to help with the cutting out in this case.

Cat puzzle

49

Clown Golf
Game

What you need :-

A large cardboard carton.
Scissors.
Pencil.
Paints & paint brush.
Golf balls and a
golf club.

1. Cut the flaps off the cardboard carton.

2. Turn the carton upside down. Draw three clowns' heads with mouths wide open on the side of the carton.

3. Cut holes in the mouths of the clowns making them three different sizes and all big enough to let a golf ball go through easily.

4. Paint the carton and the clowns' heads very brightly.

5. Put numbers above the holes, the higher numbers should be near the smaller holes.

6. Each player takes a turn to try and hit the golf balls into the holes and adds up the score. The player with the highest score is the winner. This can also be played in teams.

A Hoopla Game

What you need :-
A large flat cardboard box (a shirt box is ideal).
Scissors. Newspapers.
Paint and a brush.
Wooden clothes pegs.
Adhesive tape.
A felt tipped pen.
Rubber rings.

This game is excellent for hand and eye co-ordination in young children.

1.   Fill the box with old newspapers to make it solid then stick the lid to the bottom of the box .

2.   Paint the box as brightly as possible. Leave to dry.

3.   Cut 10 small holes in the box lid leaving an even space between each hole.

4.   Gently press a wooden clothes peg into each hole.

5.   Write the numbers from 1 to 10 underneath each peg. The game is now ready to play.

Parent's Handy Hints :-
Let the children stand at a distance from the box and take turns throwing the rubber rings over the pegs. Add the score after 6 throws each.

Egg Box Tiddlywinks Game

What you need :-

Several tiddlywink counters (or make your own from stiff cardboard).

A clean egg box.

Gummed paper.

Paper & pencil for scoring.

A felt tipped pen.

Parent's Handy Hints :-

The game is to flip the tiddlywink counters into the eggbox by pressing them with another counter. Each child has 4 turns at flipping – then the score is worked out by doing the sums –

eg. if ×2 drops into the cup numbered 3 then the score = 6.

1. Cut small circles from the gummed paper to fit the tiddlywinks, then stick them on to the counters.

2. Write a sum on each counter, e.g. +8 −7 x2 etc.

3. With the felt-tipped pen, write a number inside each cup of the egg box.

4. Take turns to flip the tiddlywink into the egg box, using another tiddlywink to do this. Add up your score after 4 flips.

Painted Pasta Necklace

What you need :-
Raffia.
Different shaped pasta pieces.
Poster paints.
Newspapers.

Parent's Handy Hint:-
Raffia is available at most craft shops.

1. Cut a length of raffia long enough to fit comfortably around your neck and leaving enough to tie a bow at the back.

2. Thread the different shapes of pasta along the raffia to make an interesting pattern.

3. Take a small piece of raffia and tie one end tightly to the middle of the front of the necklace.

4. Slot more pasta pieces on this, keeping to the pattern you have chosen, and tie a knot at the other side of your middle piece of pasta. Push the knots inside the pasta to hide them.

5. Cover a table with newspaper and paint with poster paints, being sure the back and front of the necklace is well covered. Hang it up to dry.

Bound Paper Necklace

1. Roll several paper handkerchiefs into small hard balls. Wind the cord tightly around the balls in several directions and secure tightly with a knot.

Parent's Handy Hints :-
Lovely presents can be made by your child, just using tinsel cord and a box of paper handkerchiefs.

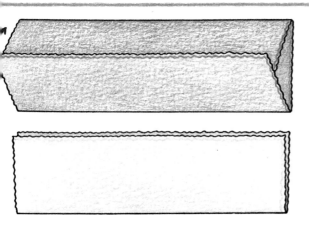
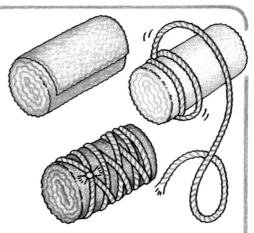

2. Make cylindrical shapes from some of the paper handkerchiefs by rolling them into rectangular strips. Bind with cord in the same way as the paper handkerchief balls.

3. Thread the cord into a large darning needle and slot the balls and the cylinders alternately mixing and matching the different shades. Tie with a bow around the back of the neck.

A Cotton Spool Belt

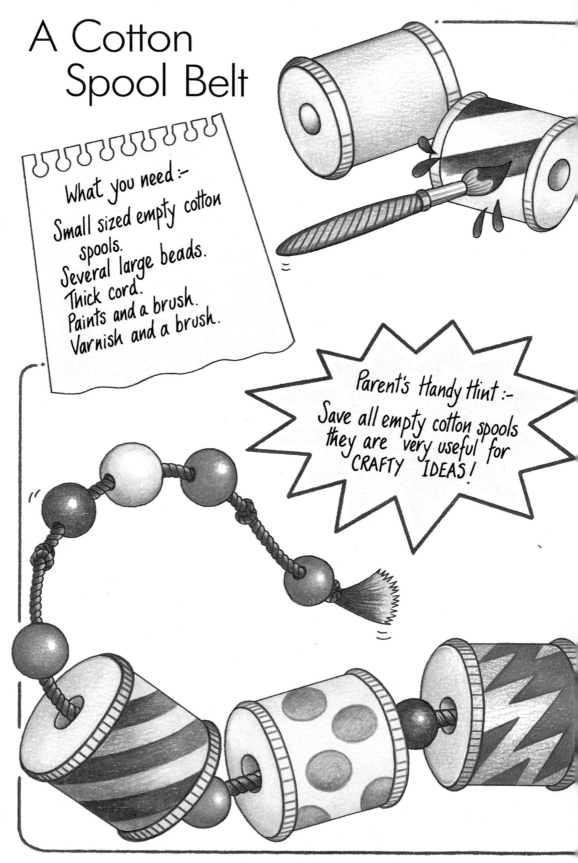

What you need :-
Small sized empty cotton spools.
Several large beads.
Thick cord.
Paints and a brush.
Varnish and a brush.

Parent's Handy Hint :-
Save all empty cotton spools they are very useful for CRAFTY IDEAS !

1. Paint the cotton reels as bright as possible. Leave to dry.

2. Varnish the reels and leave to dry.

3. Cut the cord to fit around your waist, leaving some extra for tying.

4. Tie a large knot at one end of the cord then thread the spools alternately with the beads (first a bead then a spool). Tie another knot to finish off the belt, leaving some cord to use as a fastener.

Dancer's Cone Head-dress

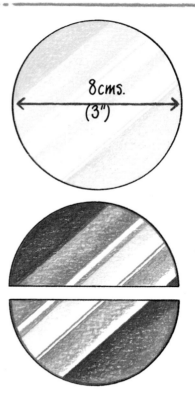

8cms.
(3")

What you need :-
Bright double - sided
foil.
Strong glue.
Tinsel cord.
Thin darning needle.

1.   Draw a circle 8cm (3") in diameter on the foil. Cut out and then cut the circle in half. This makes two semi-circles.

2.   Take one of the semi-circles, place the straight edge at the top and fold down the top left hand corner to the middle of the bottom. Repeat with the other side so that the two sides overlap. Glue together, using a strong glue, to make a cone.

3.   Thread a long, thin darning needle with the cord. Push the needle through the point of the cone leaving 20cm (8") of cord to use as a fastener. Secure the cone with a double knot. Leave 4cm (1½") of cord then thread the next cone remembering to knot it tightly at the top by passing the needle through the loop. Continue making cones until your head-dress is the right size for you.

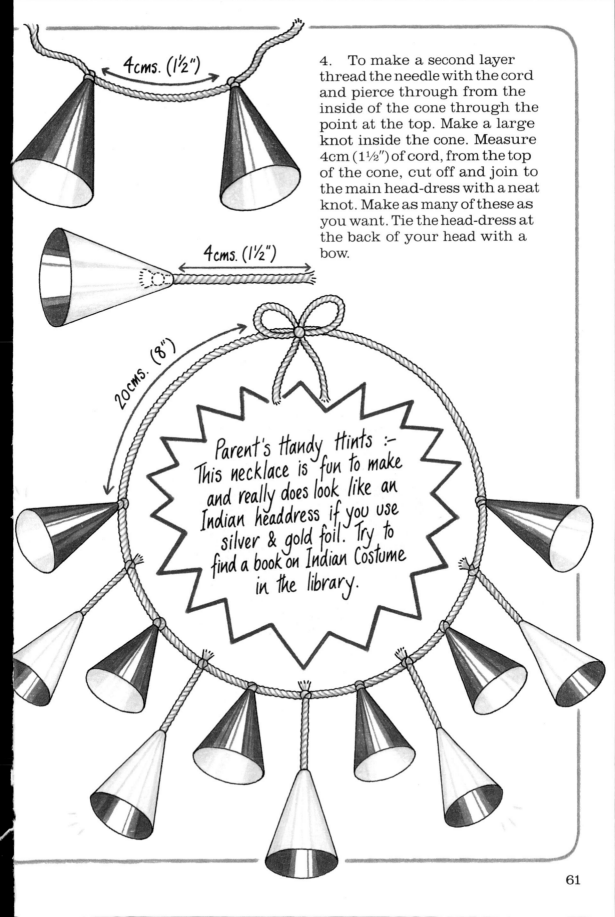

4cms. (1½")

4cms. (1½")

4. To make a second layer thread the needle with the cord and pierce through from the inside of the cone through the point at the top. Make a large knot inside the cone. Measure 4cm (1½") of cord, from the top of the cone, cut off and join to the main head-dress with a neat knot. Make as many of these as you want. Tie the head-dress at the back of your head with a bow.

20cms. (8")

Parent's Handy Hints :-
This necklace is fun to make and really does look like an Indian headdress if you use silver & gold foil. Try to find a book on Indian Costume in the library.

French Knitting

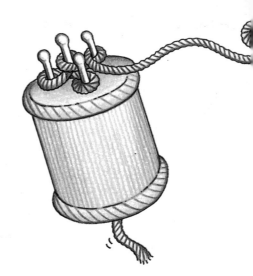

What you need :-

A cotton spool.
Left-over pieces of wool.
4 small round headed nails.
A crochet hook.
Darning needle.

4. Now as you come to each nail lift the loop below the wool over the head of the nail with the crochet hook and let it drop into the middle of the spool.

5. After you have done this a few times, pull the knitting down through the hole to make the knitting "grow" down the spool.

6. When you have made the knitting as long as you want, cast off by breaking the wool. Lift the loop off each nail in turn and pass the end of the wool through each loop, then pull tight.

1. Carefully hammer four small nails on one end of the spool, forming a small square.

2. Push the end of your wool through the hole in the spool.

3. Hold the end of the wool and the spool in one hand, and loop the wool over each of the nails in turn, turning the spool from right to left as you do so. When you get back to the first nail, do not make any more loops but still continue winding the wool on the nails just above the loops.

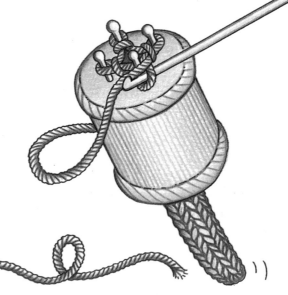